HAL•LEONARD

JAZZ PLAY ALONG®

Book and CD for B♭, E♭, C and Bass Clef Instruments

volume 42

Arranged by
Gerry Mulligan

8 JAZZ CLASSICS

BOOK

TITLE	PAGE NUMBERS			
	C Treble Instruments	B♭ Instruments	E♭ Instruments	C Bass Instruments
Bark for Barksdale	4	20	34	50
Dragonfly	6	22	36	52
Elevation	18	19	48	49
Idol Gossip	8	24	38	54
Jeru	10	26	40	56
The Lonely Night (Night Lights)	12	28	42	58
Rock Salt a/k/a/ Rocker	14	30	44	60
Theme for Jobim	16	32	46	62

CD

TITLE	CD Track Number Split Track / Melody	CD Track Number Full Stereo Track
Bark for Barksdale	1	2
Dragonfly	3	4
Elevation	5	6
Idol Gossip	7	8
Jeru	9	10
The Lonely Night (Night Lights)	11	12
Rock Salt a/k/a/ Rocker	13	14
Theme for Jobim	15	16
B♭ Tuning Notes		17

Cover photo by Franca Rota Mulligan

ISBN-13: 978-0-6340-8960-2
ISBN-10: 0-6340-8960-9

HAL•LEONARD®
CORPORATION

7777 W. BLUEMOUND RD. P.O. BOX 13819 MILWAUKEE, WI 53213

Visit Hal Leonard Online at
www.halleonard.com

GERRY MULLIGAN FAVORITES

Volume 42

Arranged by Gerry Mulligan

Featured Players:

Scott Silbert-Baritone Saxophone
Ted Rosenthal-Piano
Dean Johnson-Bass
Ron Vincent-Drums

HOW TO USE THE CD:

Each song has <u>two</u> tracks:

1) Split Track/Melody

Woodwind, Brass, Keyboard, and **Mallet Players** can use this track as a learning tool for melody style and inflection.

Bass Players can learn and perform with this track – remove the recorded bass track by turning down the volume on the LEFT channel.

Keyboard and **Guitar Players** can learn and perform with this track – remove the recorded piano part by turning down the volume on the RIGHT channel.

2) Full Stereo Track

Soloists or **Groups** can learn and perform with this accompaniment track with the RHYTHM SECTION only.

BARK FOR BARKSDALE

CD
❶ : SPLIT TRACK/MELODY
❷ : FULL STEREO TRACK

BY GERRY MULLIGAN

C VERSION

FAST SWING, IN TWO

SOLOS (6 FULL CHORUSES – LAST CHORUS FEATURES PIANO & DRUM SOLOS)

DRAGONFLY

BY GERRY MULLIGAN

IDOL GOSSIP

BY GERRY MULLIGAN

CD

7: SPLIT TRACK/MELODY
8: FULL STEREO TRACK

C VERSION

MED. SWING

TO CODA

9

SOLOS (4 CHORUSES)

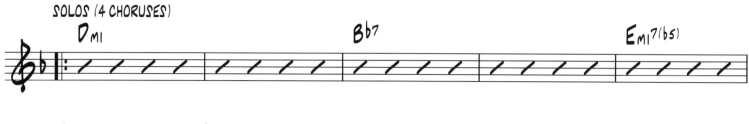

CODA

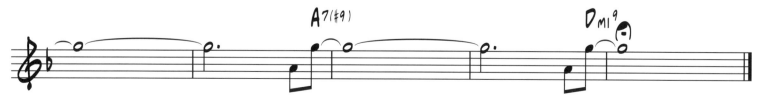

JERU

CD
◆ 9 : SPLIT TRACK/MELODY
◆ 10 : FULL STEREO TRACK

BY GERRY MULLIGAN

C VERSION

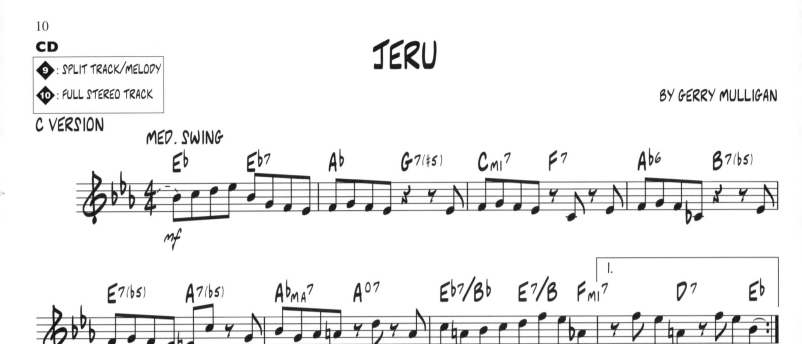

CD

THE LONELY NIGHT
(NIGHT LIGHTS)

WORDS BY JUDY HOLLIDAY
MUSIC BY GERRY MULLIGAN

C VERSION

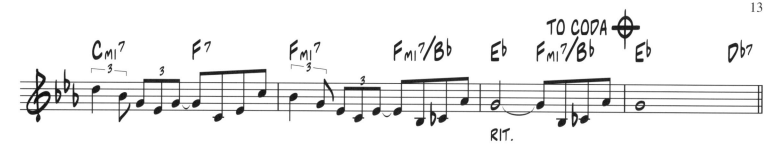

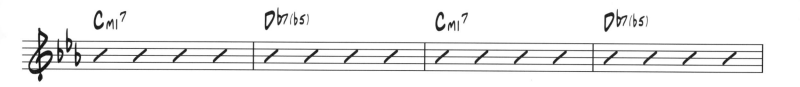

CD

15 : SPLIT TRACK/MELODY
16 : FULL STEREO TRACK

THEME FOR JOBIM

BY GERRY MULLIGAN

C VERSION

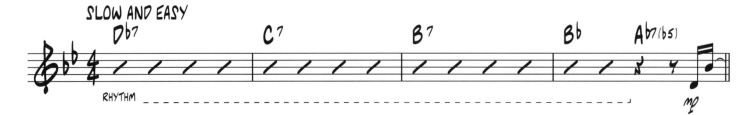

ELEVATION

ELEVATION

BY GERRY MULLIGAN AND
ELLIOT LAWRENCE

Bb VERSION   MED. FAST SWING

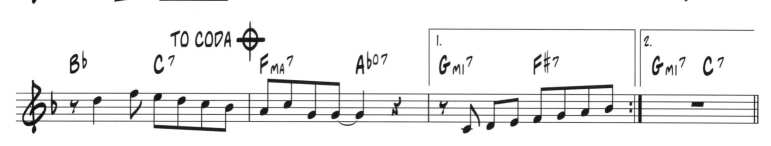

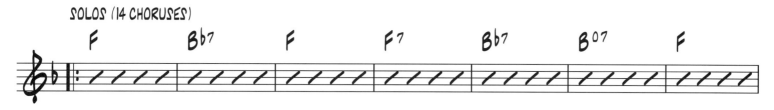

SOLOS (14 CHORUSES)

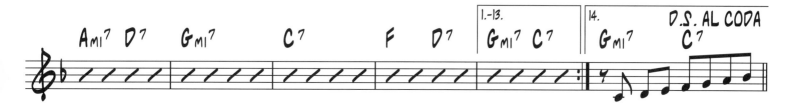

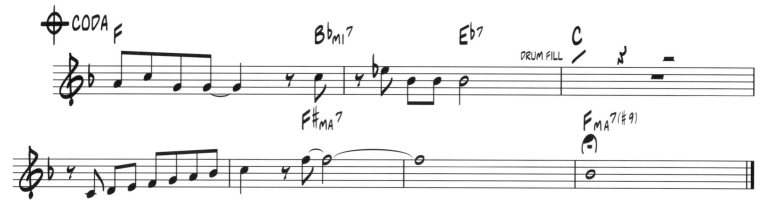

BARK FOR BARKSDALE

BY GERRY MULLIGAN

B♭ VERSION

FAST SWING, IN TWO

DRAGONFLY

BY GERRY MULLIGAN

23

IDOL GOSSIP

CD
7: SPLIT TRACK/MELODY
8: FULL STEREO TRACK

BY GERRY MULLIGAN

Bb VERSION

MED. SWING

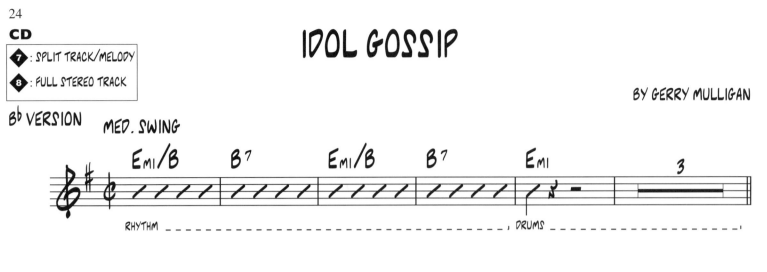

TO CODA

25

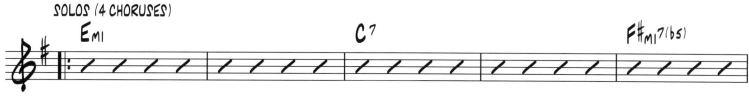

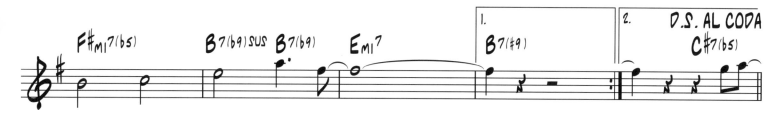

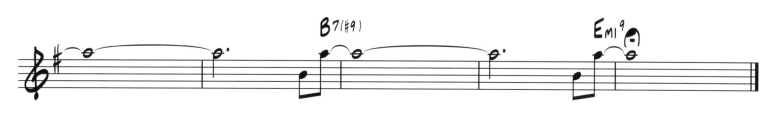

JERU

BY GERRY MULLIGAN

CD

🔟 : SPLIT TRACK/MELODY

🔢 : FULL STEREO TRACK

THE LONELY NIGHT
(NIGHT LIGHTS)

WORDS BY JUDY HOLLIDAY
MUSIC BY GERRY MULLIGAN

B♭ VERSION

SLOW AND EASY

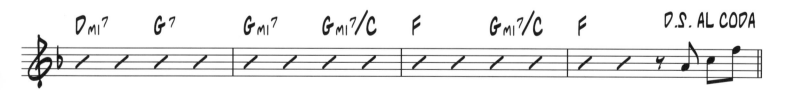

ROCK SALT
A/K/A ROCKER

BY GERRY MULLIGAN

THEME FOR JOBIM

BY GERRY MULLIGAN

Bb VERSION

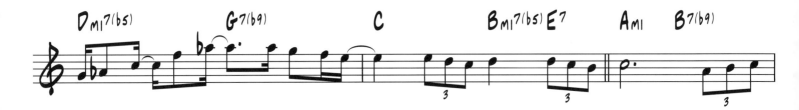

BARK FOR BARKSDALE

BY GERRY MULLIGAN

CD
1 : SPLIT TRACK/MELODY
2 : FULL STEREO TRACK

Eb VERSION

FAST SWING, IN TWO

SOLOS (6 FULL CHORUSES - LAST CHORUS FEATURES PIANO & DRUM SOLOS)

DRAGONFLY

BY GERRY MULLIGAN

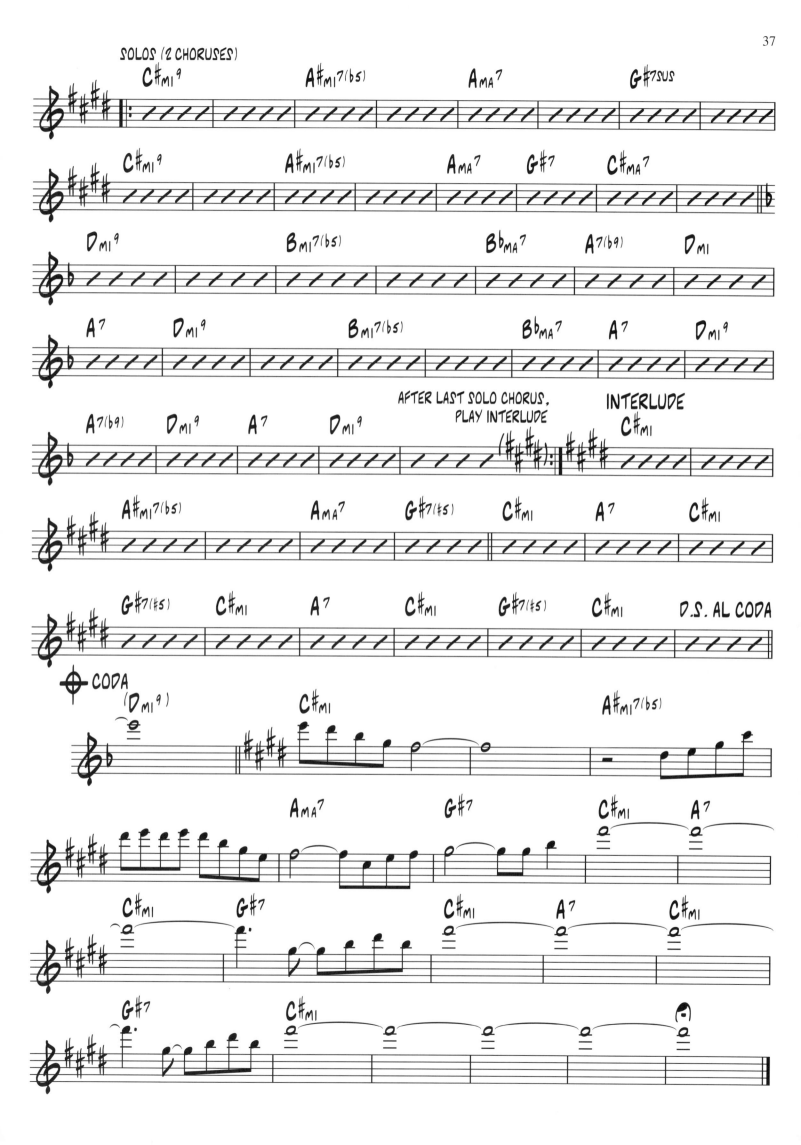

CD

7 : SPLIT TRACK/MELODY
8 : FULL STEREO TRACK

IDOL GOSSIP

BY GERRY MULLIGAN

E♭ VERSION   MED. SWING

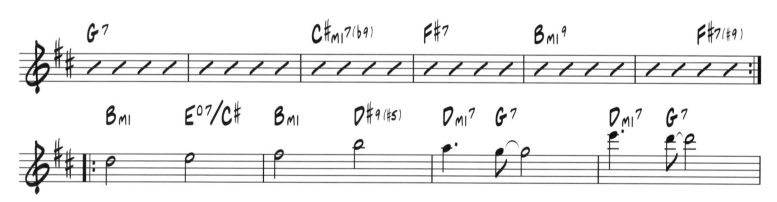

JERU

BY GERRY MULLIGAN

THE LONELY NIGHT
(NIGHT LIGHTS)

WORDS BY JUDY HOLLIDAY
MUSIC BY GERRY MULLIGAN

Eb VERSION

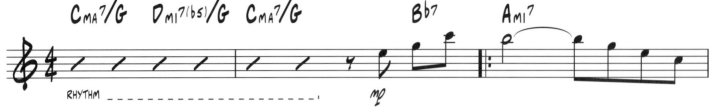

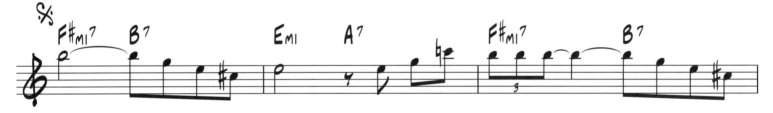

ROCK SALT
A/K/A ROCKER

BY GERRY MULLIGAN

CD
- **15**: SPLIT TRACK/MELODY
- **16**: FULL STEREO TRACK

THEME FOR JOBIM

BY GERRY MULLIGAN

Eb VERSION

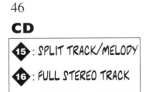
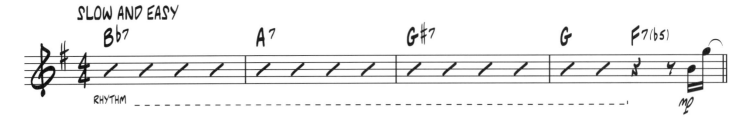

ELEVATION

ELEVATION

BY GERRY MULLIGAN AND
ELLIOT LAWRENCE

BARK FOR BARKSDALE

BY GERRY MULLIGAN

𝄢: C VERSION

FAST SWING, IN TWO

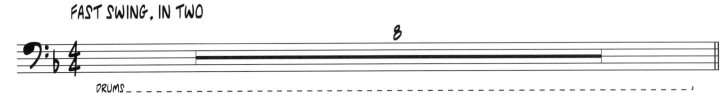

DRAGONFLY

BY GERRY MULLIGAN

CD

■ : SPLIT TRACK/MELODY
◆ : FULL STEREO TRACK

IDOL GOSSIP

BY GERRY MULLIGAN

𝄢 : C VERSION

MED. SWING

SOLOS (4 CHORUSES)

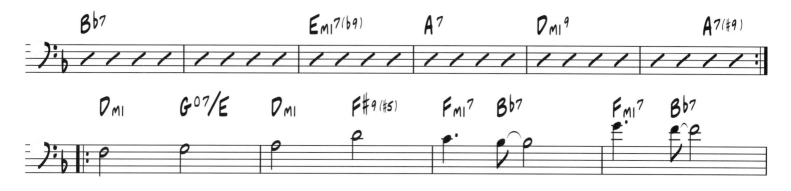

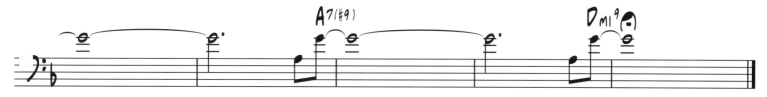

JERU

BY GERRY MULLIGAN

THE LONELY NIGHT
(NIGHT LIGHTS)

CD
11 : SPLIT TRACK/MELODY
12 : FULL STEREO TRACK

WORDS BY JUDY HOLLIDAY
MUSIC BY GERRY MULLIGAN

𝄢: C VERSION

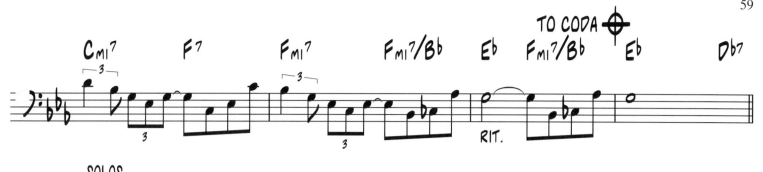

ROCK SALT
A/K/A ROCKER

BY GERRY MULLIGAN

CD
- ◆15 : SPLIT TRACK/MELODY
- ◆16 : FULL STEREO TRACK

THEME FOR JOBIM

BY GERRY MULLIGAN

𝄢 : C VERSION

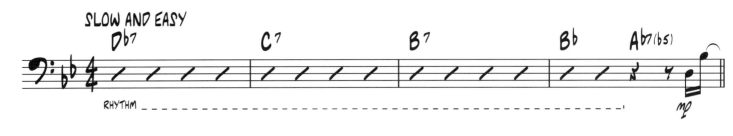